Develop

DEFORESTATION

Richard Spilsbury

WAYLAND

First published in 2011 by Wayland
Copyright © 2011 Wayland

Wayland
338 Euston Road
London NW1 3BH

Wayland Australia
Level 17/207 Kent Street
Sydney NSW 2000

Editor: Nicola Edwards
Designer: Elaine Wilkinson
Proofreader: Hayley Fairhead
Map illustrators: Ian Thompson and Adrian Stuart

Spilsbury, Richard, 1963-
  Deforestation. -- (Development or destruction?)
  1. Deforestation--Juvenile literature.
  2. Deforestation--Case studies--Juvenile literature.
  3. Forest management--Juvenile literature.
  4. Forest management--Case studies--Juvenile literature.
  I. Title II. Series
  333.7'7513-dc22

ISBN 978 0 7502 6602 4

Picture acknowledgements:

The author and publisher would like to thank the following agencies for allowing these pictures to be reproduced:

Cover: iStock © Ivoman; title page: Shutterstock; contents page: Shutterstock © Juriah Mosin; p6 © Chris Sattlberger/cultura/Corbis; p7: iStock © Ivoman; p8 (t) Shutterstock © Naaman Abreu, (b) Shutterstock © Juriah Mosin; p10 (t) Shutterstock © AridOcean, (b) Shutterstock © Tristan Tan; p11 Sutanta Aditya/AFPGetty Images; p12 Paula Bronstein/Getty Images; p13 AFP/AFP/Getty Images; p14 Robert Nickelsberg/Getty Images; p15 Shutterstock © Tristan Tan; p16 Bloomberg via Getty Images; p17 (t) Shutterstock © Oleksiy Mark, (b) Shutterstock © Atlaspix; p18 © Mark Bryan Makela/In Pictures/Corbis; p19 Bloomberg via Getty Images; p20 Shutterstock © Alexey Bykov; p21 Shutterstock © Max Blain; p22 Shutterstock © AridOcean; p23 Ami Vitale/Getty Images; p24 AFP/Getty Images; p25 AFP/Getty Images; p26 AFP/Getty Images; p27 Shutterstock © Paul Prescott; p28 (t) Shutterstock © AridOcean, (b) Shutterstock © Four Oaks; p29 Shutterstock © H&B; p30 AFP/Getty Images; p31 China Photos/Getty Images; p32 (t) Artyom Korotayev/AFP/Getty Images, (b) Natalia Kolesnikova/AFP/Getty Images; p34 Evaristo Sa/AFP/Getty Images; p35 (t) Shutterstock © guentermanaus, (b) Shutterstock © worldswildlifewonders; Mauricio Lima/AFP/Getty Images; p37 Zubin Shroff/Getty Images; p38 Time & Life Pictures/Getty Images; p39 Shutterstock © Frontpage; p40 Getty Images; p41 (t) Shutterstock © Trinh Le Nguyen, (b) Eye of Science/Science Photo Library; p42 Michael Melford/National Geographic/Getty Images; p43 Shutterstock © David Hyde

Note: The website addresses (URLs) included in this book were valid at the time of going to press. However, because of the nature of the Internet, it is possible that some addresses may have changed, or sites may have changed or closed down since publication. While the author and publishers regret any inconvenience this may cause to the readers, no responsibility for any such changes can be accepted by either the author or the publishers.

Printed in China

Wayland is a division of Hachette Children's Books,
an Hachette UK company.
www.hachette.co.uk

Contents

Forests cover about a quarter of the land area of our planet. They are important not only for their biodiversity, but also their resources. Deforestation means clearing forest or woodland to access resources such as timber and space for other activities including farming.

◁ Fields are encroaching on forest worldwide, such is the high demand for farmland and farmed products.

Deforestation in the past

Half of the USA, almost all of Europe, and much of the rest of the world were once forested. Over the last 8,000 years, human activity has removed half the original global forest cover. In the past, just as today, people cleared trees to create land for growing crops or raising livestock, and for houses and settlements. Timber was used for fuel and construction but also for trade, leading to the development of regions and countries. For example, Canadian East Coast settlements developed in the 19th century partly owing to trade in tall, straight timber from local trees that were prized as masts on British ships.

Destruction fact

The deforestation rate in the Midwest USA during the 19th and early 20th centuries was around 2 per cent of the total area each year, which is about the same as the deforestation rate in the Amazon today.

Globally deforestation has increased in scale and speed in recent centuries owing to growing populations demanding more land and timber, and growing global trade. A major reason that European countries colonized and deforested tropical regions of South America and Africa was access to valuable forest resources such as hardwoods.

Deforestation and development today

There is a strong link between deforestation and producing goods for export. In tropical countries major drivers of deforestation are clearing land for raising cattle to supply beef for global markets, as in Brazil, or growing palm trees to supply palm oil, as in Malaysia. Slow-growing tropical hardwoods for timber and wood products such as plywood are also important exports. In countries such as Finland and Canada boreal forests are felled for softwood used in construction or for wood pulp used to make paper and other products.

Deforestation is also caused by development of non-forest industries – for example, clearing land for mining of valuable metals or building pipelines to carry oil or gas. However, 40 per cent of wood taken from forests worldwide is used as fuelwood, the only affordable energy resource for many poor people.

◁ **Logging is one of the major causes of deforestation in the Amazon rainforest in Brazil.**

Importance of forest

Forests are vital resources for the whole planet. Trees, like other green plants, use carbon dioxide gas from air to make their food by photosynthesis. Carbon dioxide traps heat in the atmosphere and therefore trees help control global climates. Photosynthesis also releases oxygen which most living things need to survive. Tree roots and forest floors trap and soak up rainwater, and top up supplies in rivers, lakes and groundwater. Forests have been the source of vital medicines, such as heart drugs made from forest plants, and are important for recreation. They are vital habitats. Most land species live in forests, but tropical forests are especially biodiverse – they cover around 6 per cent of land yet contain 80 per cent of all insect species and two thirds of all plant species – and new species are discovered each year.

Spider monkeys spend their lives in high rainforest trees. They swing between trees as fast as a human can run.

Scarlet and blue and yellow macaws travel in groups through rainforest and nest in holes high in the trees.

Explore further

Find out what new species were discovered on the Foja Mountains, Indonesian New Guinea, in 2008 or on Mount Bosav Papua New Guinea, in 2009.

ON THE SCENE

'Forests are being destroyed at an alarming rate ... by doing so we are destroying our own capacity to survive.'

Olivier Langrand, Conservation International's international policy chief

▽ **This book's international case studies, located on the map below (which also shows the global distribution of different types of forest), consider the impacts of deforestation in the past, present and future.**

Problems of deforestation

Deforestation transforms habitats for wildlife, so they may struggle to find food, water or mates. When people clear land quickly by burning remaining tree stumps and waste, this can cause destructive forest fires. Cleared forest land also degrades quickly because rain washes fertile topsoil away. This means people can no longer grow crops on it after a few years of farming and may then deforest new areas. Burning trees and clearing forest soils releases greenhouse gases including carbon dioxide, and with less forest, less carbon dioxide is removed through photosynthesis. As a result, global average temperatures are rising, so deforestation is causing climate change.

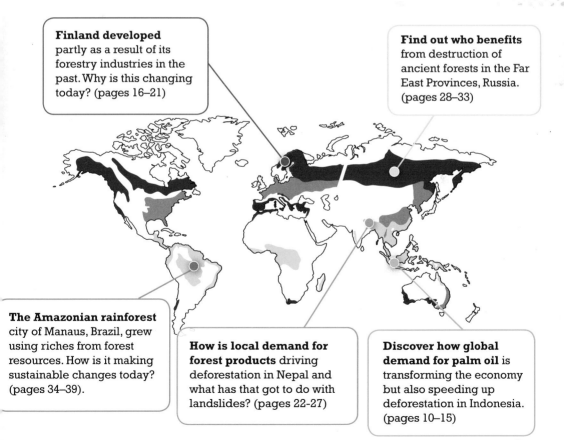

Finland developed partly as a result of its forestry industries in the past. Why is this changing today? (pages 16–21)

Find out who benefits from destruction of ancient forests in the Far East Provinces, Russia. (pages 28–33)

The Amazonian rainforest city of Manaus, Brazil, grew using riches from forest resources. How is it making sustainable changes today? (pages 34–39).

How is local demand for forest products driving deforestation in Nepal and what has that got to do with landslides? (pages 22-27)

Discover how global demand for palm oil is transforming the economy but also speeding up deforestation in Indonesia. (pages 10–15)

■ **Boreal forest**　■ **Temperate forest**　■ **Mediterranean forest**　■ **Tropical forest**

The oil-rich fruit of the oil palm, a tree that originally came from Africa, is at the centre of an important Indonesian export industry. How did the Indonesian oil palm industry emerge and does its development have to cause further deforestation?

△ Indonesia's main palm oil plantations are on the islands of Sumatra and Kalimantan.

A versatile oil

Oil palms grow small red and black fruit in clusters weighing around 50 kg. The ripe flesh is pressed to release reddish oil. Palm seeds are the world's most productive oil seeds, releasing around 6000 litres per hectare of crop or around 30 times the amount from the same area of corn. Most palm oil is used in a vast range of foods, for example as oil for frying, in margarines as spreads or in baked products, and in ice cream and coffee creamer. Palm oil is an important ingredient in many non-food substances such as soap, shampoo, cosmetics, candles and paints. It can be used as a substitute for diesel fuel in vehicles.

The palm oil industry

Oil palms were first introduced to Indonesia in the mid-19th century as ornamental plants. In 1905 a Belgian scientist noticed that the palms in Indonesia grew quicker and bore fruit higher in oil than they did in Africa. Farmers soon realized that palm oil could be a lucrative crop on the rich soils and in the warm, damp climate across the Indonesian islands, and the first palm oil plantations were created in 1917. Much more oil palm was planted in the 1920s to 1930s when global demand for natural rubber, an important Indonesian export, fell. New chemical processes had been invented that made cheaper synthetic rubber.

△ An Indonesian palm oil plantation.

Chapter 2

Destruction fact

From 1990 to 2000 the area of land devoted to palm oil production tripled in Indonesia from 1 to 3 million hectares. By 2020 the Indonesian government plans to increase this to 11 million hectares, which is nearly half the size of the UK.

Palm oil expansion

Palm oil in Indonesia

— Indonesia - Production
— Indonisia - Export

Million metric tons

18
16
14
12
10
8
6
4
2
0

1964 1967 1970 1973 1976 1979 1982 1985 1988 1991 1994 2000 2003 2006

Year

Global demand for palm oil increased after World War II for many reasons, such as that people were eating more processed foods and growing populations in Asia in particular needed more cooking oil. Immense plantations grew especially through Sumatra and Kalimantan. Today Indonesia exports around 40 per cent of global palm oil worth US$14.5 billion and the industry provides jobs for around 2 million people.

In the 1980s the Indonesian government paid millions of farmers from Java, which had little farmland and mostly undisturbed forest, to settle on less populated islands such as Sumatra. In return they would clear forest and grow palm oil to increase the country's exports. This graph shows how palm oil production and exports rose from the 1980s as a result.

▽ **A worker harvests bunches of ripe oil palm seeds in Aceh, Indonesia.**

Disappearing orangutans

The push for more palm oil is causing severe environmental damage affecting many forest species, notably the orangutan. This great ape only survives in the wild on Borneo and Sumatra. Since the 1980s around 80 per cent of orangutan habitat has disappeared due to oil plantations as well as logging and farming. Orangutans need a large range to find sufficient fruit to eat. Deforestation forces them into smaller patches of habitat crowded with more orangutans, with less food, and this can result in fewer young surviving. With fewer large trees adults are forced to move across the ground rather than swing amongst the branches and this makes them more vulnerable to predators and poachers. Orangutans disorientated by forest fires may move onto plantation land where farmers often shoot them for fear of attack.

Sumatran orangutan populations have fallen by over 86 per cent since 1900 and there may be just 7,000 left. Bornean populations are larger but still threatened by the rate of deforestation. Many other species such as the Sumatran rhinoceros and elephant, as well as forest peoples including the Dyak are also severely affected by loss of forest.

Baby orangutans orphaned when their mothers died during deforestation are cared for in a Kalimantan national park.

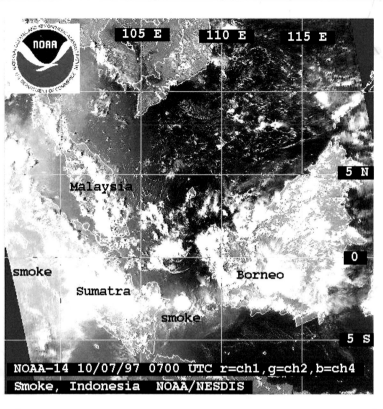

NOAA-14 10/07/97 0700 UTC r=ch1,g=ch2,b=ch4
Smoke, Indonesia NOAA/NESDIS

A satellite photo taken in early October 1997 shows the extent of smoke (yellow haze) from forest fires in Indonesia.

Atmospheric impacts

Deforestation in Indonesia partly for plantations is also having a major atmospheric impact. Farmers illegally burn tree remains on deforested patches and even set fire to standing trees to clear land faster. Fires devastate forests each year, especially in dry years. For example, deliberate fires set on over 100 plantations contributed to fires burning an area roughly three times the size of Wales between 1997 and 1998 across Indonesia. The smoke caused haze from Sri Lanka to the Philippines and polluting smog across cities in Indonesia and Malaysia. Hundreds of thousands of people were hospitalized with breathing problems and the fires caused around US$9 billion in economic, social and environmental damage.

Burning forest releases carbon dioxide into the atmosphere, contributing to global warming. The quantity of greenhouse gases released is increased when forest is cleared from damp peatland soils, found especially on Borneo and Sumatra. When peatland dries following draining and clearing, it decomposes over a long period releasing carbon dioxide and methane greenhouse gases. Also, as dry peat is a fuel, fires can burn and smoulder underground for years after surface fires are extinguished.

Destruction fact

Each hectare of peatland drained to create palm oil plantations releases around 4,500 tonnes of carbon dioxide over 25 years.

Changing the palm oil industry

Indonesia has come under a lot of international pressure to change its palm oil industry, both from other governments and from environmental groups concerned about the impact of deforestation and especially of global warming. In 2007 the Indonesian government banned clearance of peatland for plantations and in 2008 Indonesian palm oil companies agreed to stop clearing forest for new plantations and develop unforested, scrub areas (known as 'idle land') instead. The major transnational company Unilever even boycotted buying palm oil for its products from two major Indonesian companies owing to their unsustainable use of land. However, such is the demand for land from palm oil growers that the Indonesian government allowed clearance on certain areas with shallow peat from 2011.

Find out how areas are currently being sold and deforested in other countries including Congo by foreign companies hoping to profit from planting biofuel crops. What are the advantages of growing jatropha (left) to produce oil over palm trees?

▽ **A farmer tends oil palm seedlings which will be planted on land not suitable for farming as part of a conservation project promoting sustainable oil production in Indonesia.**

The fruits of the oil palm.

Need for palm oil

The palm oil industry contributes about one twentieth of Indonesia's GDP so it is not in the country's economic interests to reduce production. Demand for palm oil as biofuel has increased in recent years because crude oil is gradually running out and becoming more expensive globally. Planting oil palm helps many Indonesian farmers escape from poverty because they can earn more by selling palm oil than from food crops. But when farmers depend on export crops they grow less food. This can lead to food shortages and rising prices, and makes the farmers vulnerable to changes in the world demand for palm oil.

Development or Destruction?

Development:

* Palm oil is Indonesia's top agricultural export and the country is the world's leading supplier.
* Government subsidies for small plantation farmers have created employment for numerous smallholders in less populated parts of Indonesia.
* Indonesia is increasingly controlling the areas on which oil palm plantations can be established, for example avoiding certain areas of peatland.

Destruction:

* Global demand for palm oil for foods and for biofuels is putting pressure on Indonesia to expand plantations.
* Deforestation in Indonesia for plantations causes loss of biodiversity and forest fires.
* Deforestation on peatlands contributes more to global warming than deforestation of tropical forest in general.

Pulp industry, Finland

How can Finland's forestry industry remove 2 per cent of forest cover each year while the total forest area in this northern European country is increasing? Forestry management ensures a constant supply of wood for important Finnish export industries, such as producing wood pulp to make paper and other products. Yet changes in global demand are forcing the forestry industry to gradually change, too.

△ The Finnish forestry industry is highly mechanised for rapid processing of trees into pulp.

Finnish forest

Trees that naturally dominate in the boreal forest of Finland are conifers such as pines and spruce. These evergreen trees have waxy, needle-shaped leaves that survive the cold winters and also retain water, which is in short supply for trees when the ground is frozen. Deforestation in Finland in the past, especially in the 17th and 18th centuries, was caused mostly by clearing land for agriculture, processing trees into pitch tar, used on boats, and logging. In the 19th century the Finnish government started to regenerate deforested areas, partly to supply wood for export industries. Regenerated areas generally have closely replanted areas of pine or spruce, which are managed, by clearing weeds and thinning out weak trees, and left to grow for 60–120 years before they are big enough to harvest.

Chapter 3

History of Finnish pulp

Forestry products make up around 20 per cent of the value of Finnish exports, with pulp and pulp products as the most valuable of these. Wood is chipped and ground up in water or chemically treated to make pulp. Pulp is used to make paper and cardboard and in many other products, from paint thickeners to the absorbent parts of disposable nappies! One of the first pulp and paper mills in Finland was built in 1868 by the Nokianvirta river, which supplied hydropower for the factory. The company that ran this was later renamed Nokia (after the river), and was to become one of the world's leading telecommunication companies! Pulp mills spread through Finland over the following decades and the exports grew.

Development fact

Today around three-quarters of Finland is covered with forest and this is being deforested at only four-fifths of the rate at which new forest is growing.

▷ Helsinki is Finland's capital city and its main seaport, handling forestry products for export.

In the 1950s and 1960s the government wanted to use the pulp industry to expand the economy of northern Finland. They built railways and roads leading to ports so ships could export pulp and paper to the rest of Europe. This encouraged pulp companies to create mills employing many people, and communities developed near the mills. For example, Kemijaervi was a small lakeside village until the government built the mill in 1964, employing 500 people, and the village developed into a town. Companies supplying mills such as Metso, which makes pulping machines, grew as the mills expanded.

Impacts of deforestation

The Finnish forestry industry is regenerating forest, so why is deforestation an issue? The problem is that regenerated new forest can be quite different from original 'old-growth' forest. Although there may be the same species, the structure is different because new forest is managed. All trees are about the same age, closely packed to fit more into each hectare, and any dead trees are removed as they are not productive. Old-growth forest has not just some old, large trees, but also a range of different-sized trees, and some dead trees either standing or fallen. Fallen trees clear spaces in forest where small plants can grow. Fungi and beetles feed on deadwood, and birds such as the rare White-backed woodpecker may create nest holes in it.

In northern Finland, deforestation of old-growth forest has affected the lives of local Sami people and their tradition of reindeer herding. Sami families move with reindeer between different pastures where the animals feed on ground lichen. In winter, when the ground is frozen, reindeer rely on tree-hanging lichen found on old pine trees. Deforestation of old-growth forest makes it harder for the reindeer to survive. However, Finnish forestry companies are increasingly protecting areas of old-growth forest or felling fewer old trees during forest regeneration so new forest is more varied like old-growth forest.

▽ **The traditional Sami reindeer herding lifestyle in Finland is in danger of dying out before the next generation can take it on, partly as a result of deforestation.**

▽ The giant Kemijaervi pulp mill now lies empty and the Finnish pulp industry is in serious decline.

Falling demand

The problem when places develop based on export revenue from single industries is that there are few other sources of income when demand falls. The demand for Finnish pulp has fallen since the 1990s largely because more people are now reading news and articles on the Internet rather than newspapers and magazines, and because Asian countries are supplying cheaper pulp from quick-growing trees such as eucalyptus. From 2001 to 2009, the global price of pulp fell by 20 per cent.

ON THE SCENE

'When the mills are shuttered in bad times, people don't find other jobs.'

Eeero Lehto, chief economist at the Labour Institute for Economic Research, Helsinki

The world's biggest paper company Stora Enso, based partly in Finland, closed down five major Finnish mills including the one in Kemijaervi, putting thousands out of work. The population of Kemijaervi has shrunk by a third partly because many people, particularly the younger, less experienced forestry workers, have been forced to move to find work, for example in the thriving telecommunications and electronics industries based in and around Helsinki. When mill towns shrink, so does demand for services. The Finnish government closed 90 primary schools in 2008 mostly in northern Finland where the forestry industry is shrinking.

Forestry futures

	2007	2015	2020	Change 2007 vs. 2020	
				Quantity	%
Pulp and paper (million tonnes)	27.1	19.8	16.9	10.2	-37
Wood products (million m³)	14.3	11.8	11.9	2.4	-17

The Finnish Forest Research Institute predicts that demand for forestry products in future will fall, based on knowledge of population change in Europe, and changes in the global forestry industry. This table shows their forecasts of the amounts of pulp and wood products that Finland's forestry industry will produce in future.

Changing industry

The fall in demand for Finnish pulp and paper is greater than that for wood products. These include sawn softwood for construction but also high-quality plywood made from birch trees. Manufacturing these wood products creates huge amounts of sawdust and woodchip as waste. Pulp and paper mills can use up this waste to make pulp and therefore require fewer cut trees as raw material. With a shrinking pulp industry, less sawdust and woodchip is used.

The Finnish Forestry Research Institute predicts that the sawdust, waste, and also pulp could be used to expand its bioenergy industry. Biomass has been used in Finland for decades – it supplies around 20 per cent of Finland's energy mostly through combined heat and power plants. These burn black liquor, which is waste from pulp mills, and waste from sawmills to make electricity that powers mills and supply heat for communities.

In 2011 Nastola biogas production plant opened north-east of Helsinki making renewable transport fuel from wood chip. Could the pulp mills of today in Finland be transformed into biorefineries that could export fuels and other useful chemicals rather than paper and pulp?

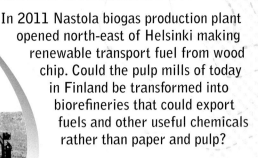

Woodchip produced in Finnish mills was once largely a raw material for the pulp industry, but is now growing in importance for use in the bioenergy industry.

Development or Destruction?

Development:

* Deforestation in Finland, mostly of forest plantations, supplies mills whose products are valuable exports for the country.

* Pulp mills have created development and provided jobs for thousands of people.

* The forestry industry is increasingly recognizing the value of and protecting old-growth forest.

* The pulp industry is impacted by changing global demand yet has the potential to reinvent itself as a biofuel industry.

Destruction:

* The forestry industry is reducing the quality if not the quantity of forests in Finland, which is affecting Sami people and wildlife.

* Regions that developed based on pulp mills are economically and socially affected by falling demand for pulp and paper.

Changing landuse

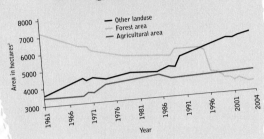

Area in hectares²

8000
7000
6000
5000
4000
3000

— Other landuse
— Forest area
— Agricultural area

1961 1966 1971 1976 1981 1986 1991 1996 2001 2004

Year

Nepal's highest mountains are too cold for trees to grow, but much of the rest of the country was once forested. Deforestation in the past and today is partly caused by demand for forest products such as fuelwood. The impacts of deforestation are being felt throughout the country.

This graph shows how the forested area of Nepal shrank from 1961 to 2004 while farmland and land for settlements increased. The sudden fall in forest area in 1994-5 is the result of changing how forest cover was assessed. Before this it was estimated from photos taken from aeroplanes and field surveys. After 1994 more accurate surveys were done using satellite images.

Forest loss

Today only around 30 per cent of Nepal's original forests remain. Probably the greatest rate of deforestation occurred between 1947 and 1980, mostly in the flat Terai region near the border with India. Few people lived in this marshy, forested region formerly because malaria, a lethal disease, was common. The government used chemicals to kill off mosquitoes, which spread malaria, to make the region more habitable.

▽ This map shows the Terai region and the mid-hills of Nepal.

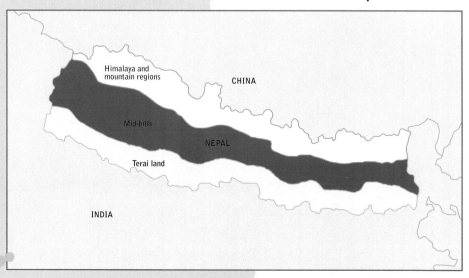

Himalaya and mountain regions

CHINA

Mid-hills

NEPAL

Terai land

INDIA

They relocated thousands of people from the crowded mid-hills to clear forest and create farmland to grow rice, their major food. The government logged valuable Terai trees to export to India. Today forest is scarce, not only in the Terai, but also across the rest of Nepal. The remaining forests are under pressure in part owing to demand from Nepalis for forest products.

The importance of forest products

Around 85 per cent of Nepalese people live in the countryside and rely on farming for their food and livelihood. Forest products are very important to these poor subsistence farmers. They use tree leaves and branches as free livestock food and bedding, and may use forest plants as medicines. Probably the most important resource is fuelwood for cooking and heating. People may cut down whole trees, or remove or collect fallen branches and twigs for fuelwood. Fuelwood supplies over 80 per cent of energy used in Nepalese homes. As the country is so deforested, many people struggle to collect all the fuelwood they need. For example, in some villages families spend an average of eight hours each day collecting sufficient fuelwood from sparse forest, and some children miss out on school as a result.

◁ **Women and children in Nepal are usually responsible for the tiring and time-consuming task of collecting and carrying fuelwood to their family homes.**

Landslides and flooding

Deforestation in Nepal is a major cause of landslides in the country. Landslides are when soil or rock slide or fall down slopes. Many occur when soil or rock soaks up rainwater and becomes so heavy that it slips over the underlying rock. The steep mountains of Nepal have thousands of landslides each year, especially during the annual monsoon season of heavy rains. Forested areas have fewer landslides than deforested areas. When rain falls, leaves retain moisture and soften the impact of raindrops on soil. Tree roots absorb moisture and help hold together soil. A study in western Nepal found that streams beneath deforested slopes contained seven times the amount of soil, from landslides, than those beneath undisturbed forest.

Landslides may destroy mountain roads, affecting transport, and villages, around which deforestation is more intense. Heavy rain runs fast off deforested slopes and can cause destructive and lethal flash floods. Rivers often flood during the monsoon in Nepal but this is made worse by landslides which can fill in or even block rivers and make them more likely to flood. Severe floods in western Nepal in 2009 affected over 100,000 people.

▽ **Local residents clear debris caused by a landslide in the mid-hills west of Kathmandu in 2003.**

24

Forests for the people

Today communities in Nepal are planting more trees on slopes to help reduce landslides and flooding as well as to supply their forest product needs. Community forests were first encouraged by the Nepalese government to help slow deforestation. In 1979, the government banned logging and protected whole areas of forest, and the wildlife living there, such as one-horned rhinos, in national parks and wildlife reserves. The trouble was that local people who had always harvested forest resources were no longer allowed in. This created resentment between locals and the government. It also led to a rise in illegal logging and poaching, partly because people could make money from helping loggers and poachers to buy necessities.

In the 1990s the government responded by giving areas of trees around protected forests to communities. In these community forests locals can harvest and benefit from forest products, and grow and replant seedling trees to replace what they have taken. The government provides ongoing funds and expertise to locals to help them manage community forests. Today community forests cover an area of 14 million hectares and benefit over 6 million people in Nepal.

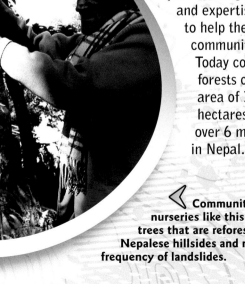

Community forest nurseries like this one grow the trees that are reforesting many Nepalese hillsides and reducing the frequency of landslides.

This Nepalese villager is cooking with biogas in her home in the south of the country.

Alternatives to fuelwood

Many communities in Nepal, especially remote ones in mountains, have limited options for fuel apart from fuelwood owing to their poverty. In order to reduce deforestation for fuelwood, the government and charities including the Worldwide Fund for Nature are helping to pay for biogas plants in parts of Nepal. Biogas plants are tanks in which bacteria break down toilet and kitchen waste and cattle manure to release methane gas that may be burnt as fuel in stoves.

For families that cannot afford biogas plants, the government is also subsidizing the cost of buying improved cooking stoves, which burn wood more efficiently than traditional stoves. Using improved stoves and biogas saves time spent on cooking and fuel collection, so women and children have more time for education. It also reduces the amount of smoke and soot indoors that previously has caused breathing problems.

Innovations

In some mountainous parts of Nepal people prepare meals on solar cookers that use no fuel. Solar cookers have wide, shiny concave dishes that are angled towards the sun. The dish shape reflects sunlight onto a cooking pan or kettle positioned in the centre and heat energy in sunlight warms the food or water. Solar cookers are especially useful within national parks where no fuelwood cutting is allowed.

Development or Destruction?

Development:

* Nepalese subsistence farmers and their families may have no other affordable options than using forest products to feed their livestock and supply domestic energy.
* Deforestation allowed settlement and development of the Terai region.
* Timber sales provided valuable income for Nepal in the past.

Destruction:

* Deforestation causes destructive landslides and floods each year in Nepal.
* Poor people in Nepal have limited options for fuel apart from fuelwood. However, using biogas, improved stoves or solar cookers supplies energy while slowing deforestation. In addition, community forests in Nepal can supply wood products such as fuelwood without deforestation.

RUSSIA

• Moscow

Boreal forest

KAZAKHSTAN

CHINA

Suifenhe •• Vladivostok

The shading on this map shows the extent of Russia's boreal forest.

The boreal forest, or taiga, stretches from Alaska across Canada and northern Europe to the Far East of Russia. The trees and animals that live in this region of Russia, thousands of kilometres from Moscow, are under threat owing to logging, yet few Russians are benefitting from timber sales.

Taiga life

The region of taiga in the southernmost part of the Far East Provinces in Russia is where conifers found in boreal forest coexist with broadleaved species such as oak and ash found in subtropical Asian forest. In total there are well over 2,000 forest species in the taiga, ranging from plants such as ginseng, to animals including mandarin ducks and black bears. The nuts from the cedar pines and acorns from the oaks are central to the taiga food chain as they are important foods for forest animals including wild boar and deer. These are key prey for the rare Amur tigers and leopards.

Amur tigers are the world's largest tiger subspecies and one of the rarest, existing in the wild only in Russia's Far East.

Taiga forest in Russia's Far East Provinces.

Chapter 5

EXPLORE FURTHER

Discover how deforestation in Sumatra (Indonesia), India and the Caspian Sea region (Russia) has affected regional and global tiger populations.

They were hunted almost to extinction up to 1947 but then officially protected along with their prey species. The pines and oaks were also protected, not least because pine nuts are also an important forest product sold for export by local people.

Indigenous taiga peoples include the Udege and Nanai. Traditionally the Udege live in small groups that roam through the forest sustainably hunting forest animals and collecting forest produce such as honey and berries.

Pressure on the forest

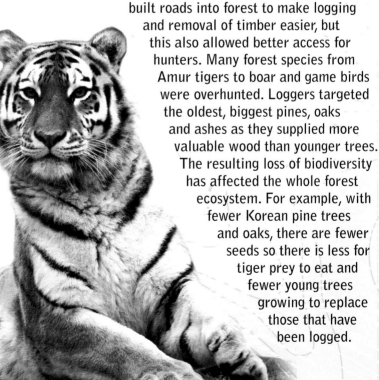

▽ Amur tiger numbers have dropped down to the current 400 or so remaining individuals largely as a result of illegal poaching, but also because of habitat and prey loss caused by deforestation.

Russia was once part of a much larger Soviet Union that broke up into individual countries in 1991. The Russian government faced economic difficulties following the break-up and state-controlled industries closed down. Regions of Russia put up many of their natural resources for sale. In the Far East these ranged from iron, tin and coal to trees. Logging companies built roads into forest to make logging and removal of timber easier, but this also allowed better access for hunters. Many forest species from Amur tigers to boar and game birds were overhunted. Loggers targeted the oldest, biggest pines, oaks and ashes as they supplied more valuable wood than younger trees. The resulting loss of biodiversity has affected the whole forest ecosystem. For example, with fewer Korean pine trees and oaks, there are fewer seeds so there is less for tiger prey to eat and fewer young trees growing to replace those that have been logged.

Russian logs for China

Chinese Imports	1997	1998	1999	2000	2001	2002	2003	2004	2005
Total logs imported from Russia	0.95	1.59	4.31	5.93	8.77	14.80	14.37	16.96	20.04
Total logs imported by China	4.46	4.82	10.14	13.61	16.86	24.33	25.46	26.24	29.37
Ratio of Russian log imports to total imports	21.27	30.99	42.47	43.57	51.98	60.86	56.44	64.63	68.25

Widespread deforestation in China during the late 20th century was held responsible for the severe flooding of the Yangtze River in 1998. The government started to protect more Chinese forest and import more logs instead. This table shows how the quantity imported and the proportion supplied by neighbouring Russia rose between 1997 and 2005.

Illegal logging

There has been a boom in illegal logging in Far East Russia since the 1990s. This has been caused largely by increasing demand for timber for export, mostly to China. The Russian government's Forest Service has lega limits on how much wood can be extracted from forests, yet has very little control over illegal logging. This is partly because there are few employees, for example the Primorsky region is the size of Florida but has just 12 forest inspectors.

However, the biggest problem is that corrupt Forest Service employees illegally auction licences to log more than the legal limit in unprotected areas. They also use loopholes in Russian law to allow loggers access to protected forest for 'sanitation logging'. Sanitation logging is cutting out sick or fallen trees to keep forests healthy, but loggers instead cut valuable, healthy old trees.

The illegal loggers are mostly Chinese immigrants but also Russians, who have few other local job options. Loggers use heavy machinery to pull down and remove trees quickly, so they are not caught in the act by the police.

▽ A train from Vladivostok in Russia arrives at the Russia-China border town of Suifenhe loaded with logs.

They mostly load the logs onto trains for export into China. The illegal loggers use false logging or harvest permits signed by corrupt Forest Service employees to get their exports past border customs officials. Some environmental groups estimate that each year 700,000 wagons full of wood are transported from Russia to China, and at least half are illegally logged.

Border development

The border region between Far East Russia and China is rapidly developing owing to the influx of Chinese businesses that have grown rich on exporting Russian wood. On the Russian side of the border, there are few Russian-owned businesses that profit from Russian timber and offer work to local people. On the Chinese side there are timber importing companies and also many sawmills. These process logs of Korean pine, Manchurian oak and other taiga species into more valuable cut timber either for direct export or for use in factories in other parts of China.

Chinese settlements near the border are growing based on trade. For example, the population of the border city of Suifenhe increased five-fold from 2000 to 2010. Many of the larger population are lowly paid migrant workers from other parts of China. They live in poor housing near the railway yard, where timber and logs are handled, while the rich bosses of the timber businesses live in luxury brick houses and drive expensive cars.

◁ Workers in a timber plant in Yanbian, China, near Vladivostok process logs into timber and furniture for export.

Further threats to forest

In 2010 taiga in the Far East of Russia was badly affected by forest fires. Environmental groups claim that the cost of reforestation and value of burnt timber was around US$300 billion.

Fires can burn fiercely through taiga in the region as the climate is quite dry and warm. They can start naturally but most in 2010 were accidentally started by people, for example from sparks produced by forestry machinery, from cigarettes, or by cooking fires left by hunters. Fires are made much worse by deforestation. Illegal loggers typically remove the valuable trunks of large trees and leave unwanted branches and thin trees on the ground.

A forest fire rages as a firefighter tries to stop the flames reaching the Russian village of Dolginino in August 2010.

People protesting in Russia against corruption leading to deforestation.

Around 30 per cent of the forest cover remains in logged areas. When fires start, they can spread rapidly across whole regions. Logging companies claim that building roads into untouched regions of forest, such as those where Udege people live, allows access to fire-fighting vehicles that can reduce destruction of valuable trees by fires. The Udege claim that new roads accelerate illegal logging and poaching.

Safeguarding forest

Opposition to illegal logging and deforestation in the Far East is growing in Russia. This is partly because of a recent TV documentary called 'Dark Forest' that exposed corruption in the forestry industry. In October 2010 public protest prevented the auction of sanitation logging permits in a protected Korean cedar pine, oak and ash forest in Primorsky province. However, without government investment in better forest management, some experts predict that the old-growth oak and ash forests of the Far East may have disappeared by 2020.

Development or Destruction?

Development:

* Deforestation is benefitting the development of Russia-China border towns that are log and timber export and processing centres.

* For unemployed Russians and migrant Chinese workers, illegal logging is an important source of income.

* There is some legal protection for rare taiga forest in Russia, and increasing public pressure against illegal logging.

Destruction:

* Deforestation is endangering rare taiga, including Korean cedar pine, oak and ash, and animals dependent on forest including Amur tigers.

* Destruction of cedar pine trees reduces pine nut harvests which are economically important for local Udege people.

* Destruction following illegal logging can increase the spread of forest fires. Forest roads built to help people put out fires may help loggers and hunters damage the taiga biome further.

Manaus, Brazilian Amazon

When most people hear the term deforestation they think of the Amazon rainforest, the largest tropical forest in the world. Manaus, deep in the forest, and Brazil as a whole have benefitted economically from deforestation in the past. However, the country is increasingly using the forest more sustainably and encouraging development without environmental destruction.

The developing city of Manaus is surrounded by dense Amazon forest.

Development of Manaus

Manaus in northwestern Brazil is the capital of the Amazonas state. It lies on the banks of the wide Rio Negro, a tributary of the Amazon. Manaus developed economically in the late 19th and early 20th centuries based largely on wealth from exporting natural rubber, tapped from rainforest trees. Boats carried rubber from Manaus to Atlantic ports along the Amazon. The rainforest city grew, with housing, a cathedral and even an opera house. Over time, demand for rubber fell and other exports took its place, some based on Amazonas natural resources such as brazil nuts and guarana, a forest fruit used to flavour fizzy drinks.

In the 1970s, deforestation throughout Amazonas and other forested states was actively encouraged by the Brazilian government to create farmland for landless people from other parts of the country and to exploit the abundant natural resources. These included timber and beef or hides from cattle reared on cleared forest land, timber such as valuable teak and rosewood trees, and gold from forest mines. Manaus's development also caused further deforestation. For example, forest was flooded to create the Balbina hydroelectric dam in the 1980s in order to supply electricity to the city's homes and businesses.

Chapter 6

⋀ ⋁ Two of the Amazon's best-known species, the pink river dolphin (above) and harpy eagle (below), the world's largest eagle, capable of hunting full-grown monkeys.

Impacts of deforestation

The Brazilian Amazon forest is vast and biodiverse. Lifeforms vary from marmosets the length of a toothbrush and pink river dolphins to vast trees and water lilies in the river. It is estimated that around 10 per cent of all the world's known species live there. The forest is so enormous it even helps to regulate the local and global atmosphere. Water recycles through the forest by evaporation and rainfall, and the trees contribute 30 per cent of oxygen in the atmosphere. Deforestation can cause droughts in the region, making areas of rainforest more susceptible to forest fires. It has caused the loss of indigenous forest peoples. For example, building the Balbina dam near Manaus forced a third of the surviving members of the Waimiri-Atroari tribe off land they had occupied for centuries. Hunting, which has been made easier by the building of roads and other causes of deforestation, has endangered several Amazon species including jaguars and harpy eagles.

Destruction fact

A total area of trees over twice the size of the UK disappeared from the Amazon rainforest between 1970 and 2010.

Industries in Manaus today

Products such as beef and timber, whose production is linked with deforestation, remain part of the Manaus economy but today there is greater diversity. For example, factories in Manaus manufacture and export the latest flatscreen TVs and mobile phones, and refine petroleum from Peruvian oil. Manaus is also the major tourism hub in the Amazon region. It is ideally situated between river and dense rainforest, and has good infrastructure including an international airport, roads, ferries and pleasure boats, and numerous hotels.

Brazilian workers construct dvd players at Philips' modern electronics factory at Manaus.

The fastest growing type of tourism around Manaus is 'ecotourism'. This is where the industry aims to be sustainable, for example by recycling waste water, benefit local conservation, and provide jobs and wages for local people. For example, locals with knowledge of the rainforest act as guides for visitors. There are several ecolodges near Manaus built mostly using local materials that offer holidays amongst the trees or by the river. They include the Ariau Jungle Towers, the world's largest treetop hotel, and the smaller Uakari Floating Lodge inside the Mamirauá Sustainable Development Reserve.

Ecotourism initiatives around Manaus enable tourists not only to stay in and experience the Amazon forest, but also to help preserve this unique biome.

Chico Mendes and his legacy

Chico Mendes was internationally well known as a defender of the rights of the poor, especially in the Brazilian Amazon. In 1988 he was killed by people working for big businesses because he was protesting at their snatching land, to deforest, from local people who sustainably farmed the forest. His legacy in Brazil includes 'extractive reserves', where people manage forest and exploit resources but in a sustainable way. For example, the Ambé project in Para state, 700km downstream from Manaus, is a protected area of forest where farmers taking part can cut down selected trees for sale in a 25-year cycle. This allows time for new trees to grow and replace them. Local families also produce jewellery from seeds, cosmetic oils from plants, and even rubber toys for sale.

Development fact

The 280 families in the Ambé project now have twice the income that they had before when they farmed on deforested land.

ON THE SCENE

'[We] have worked to save the Amazonian rainforest and to demonstrate that progress without destruction is possible.'

Chico Mendes, 1988, speech at Sao Paulo University weeks before his death

Slowing deforestation

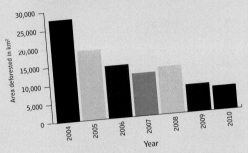

Area deforested in km² / Year
(Bar chart showing years 2004 through 2010, with values decreasing from about 28,000 in 2004 to about 11,000 in 2010. Y-axis scaled from 0 to 30,000 in increments of 5,000.)

This bar chart shows how deforestation in Brazil has fallen since 2004. Satellite images now help the government environment agency IBAMA to spot the illegal felling of trees. Officers seize the equipment of suspected illegal loggers, so they can't continue logging, and block their access to government loans, so they have to find their own money to pay fines. Deforestation is falling because of other reasons, too. For example, other countries such as the USA and Argentina are producing cheap beef so there is less demand for ranch space in Brazil.

Changing development

Brazil is the largest and richest country in South America. It is the eighth largest economy in the world yet a quarter of its people live in poverty. Many live without electricity and have little access to schools, hospitals and other infrastructure, let alone employment options. The challenge for Brazil is to develop economically, and benefit the 30 million people who live in the Amazon region, without destroying the rainforest. For example, a new road heading south from Manaus will benefit locals in being able to export their products and attract tourists, yet 75 per cent of all deforestation in the Amazon is estimated to have taken place within 50km of roads, which provide easier access for loggers.

IBAMA agents check truckers' papers to confirm whether the logs they are transporting were legally or illegally felled.

The country is a global leader in using renewable energy to supply power rather than fossil fuels, whose use creates large amounts of greenhouse gases. Half of Brazil's power is hydroelectric and the country leads world research in biofuels – 50 per cent of the fuel in Brazil's cars is ethanol made mostly from sugar cane. However, increasing demand for ethanol and biodiesel, made from soya beans, is causing further deforestation. The reason is that energy companies are buying up cheap, low-quality deforested land to grow these crops and this forces people who formerly used this land to clear farmland in the rainforest.

An area of forest a third that of Wales disappeared in Brazil in 2010, yet its rate of deforesation is falling (see panel on page 38).

Development or Destruction?

Development:

* Forest resources partly resulting from deforestation enabled Manaus to develop into the major Amazon city.
* Amazon riches have helped Brazil become a major global economy and deforestation has provided work and land for many.

Destruction:

* Deforestation for resources and space in the Brazilian Amazon has badly affected rainforest species and local, indigenous people.
* Ecotourism and extractive reserves in Amazonas are significant parts of the economy and would be harmed by future deforestation.

Sustainable futures

Future demand for wood and forest products, and farmland and resources hidden beneath the trees, is predicted to rise globally in future. Fast growing populations and economies, such as those in Africa, will put greater pressure on forests. For the great number of people in poverty around the world, forests remain vital to subsistence living. Numerous businesses and regional and national economies rely on forests for income. So how can we use the world's forest more sustainably and slow deforestation?

Development fact

Globally about 12 per cent of the total forest area is protected, but this varies by region. For example, 20 per cent of forest in North and Central America is protected compared with just 5 per cent in Europe.

Conservation

Forests are critical for maintaining the atmosphere, limiting climate change, preventing floods and landslides (see case study on page 24) and preserving biodiversity. Protecting areas of forest is vital, yet is ineffective when there are few people guarding large areas of forest (for example, see page 30). Conservation is helped for example by using improved satellite technology to more rapidly spot logging (see pages 22 and 38), but globally there needs to be greater government control over conservation.

▷ Forest rangers, as here in the USA, may have to patrol large areas of forest to protect them effectively and highlight the importance to visitors of woodland conservation.

Chapter 7

One sustainable approach to conservation is to encourage community forests or extractive reserves (see pages 25 and 36). Local people have great knowledge of forest life and resources, and are more likely to conserve them and prevent illegal logging when they can benefit, for example in jobs in ecotourism or sale of resources. Another is for commercial forest industries to manage forests, for example by leaving some old trees uncut, in order to maintain biodiversity while also extracting resources (see page 37).

△ Deforestation especially of old-growth forest continues in Vietnam, yet replanting trees nationwide increased the forested area by around 40 per cent between 1990 and 2010.

Forests and energy

Demand for some wood products such as pulp is falling yet for others such as wood for energy it is rising (see pages 20-21). Government policies in regions such as Europe and the USA are encouraging the use of renewable fuels such as biodiesel and wood to meet energy demand in order to slow greenhouse gas emissions from burning fossil fuels. Demand for biofuels is causing deforestation directly, for example the spreading palm plantations of Indonesia (see page 10), and indirectly, for example demand for soya beans in Brazil is forcing more farmers into rainforest (see page 39). However, carefully managed plantations can supply more of our energy needs without further deforestation (see page 21) and new technologies are even making it possible to harvest biofuels directly from trees (see box below).

Innovations

Scientists studying rainforests in southern Chile have discovered a fungus (left) that can make chemicals similar to diesel from wood of the tree it naturally lives on. In future scientists might be able to grow the fungus in tanks containing nutrients rather than on trees and harvest biofuel in large quantities.

Supporting change

Do you think about where wood used to make furniture, paper or other products you buy comes from? One of the best ways to prevent illegal logging is to ensure that the forest products we buy come from legal, sustainably managed plantations or forests, rather than protected or rare forests. Organizations such as the Forest Stewardship Council (FSC) and the Programme for the Endorsement of Forest Certification (PEFC) verify timber sources and label products. There are similar organizations that certify sustainable palm oil and other forest products.

Certification takes time and money as it involves inspectors visiting forests and seeing how they are managed, so certified products may cost more. This is why most wood is not certified and hence it is often unclear where it comes from and whether it was legally felled (see pages 30-31). Big companies need to take more responsibility in sourcing legal timber. For example, Ikea is the 3rd biggest wood buyer in the world. It currently sources 24 per cent of its wood from FSC plantations and works with WWF to help increase the global coverage of certified forests.

△ FSC certification in this sustainable forest management project in Guyana means that there is control over which trees can be cut down and that locals benefit from their sale.

Destruction fact

Carbon dioxide emissions from the destruction of tropical rainforests are nearly six times those from all the world's aircraft.

Pricing the living forest

Many people think that the way to slow deforestation while maintaining income for forest-rich countries such as Brazil is to make trees worth more alive than dead. Trees can be thought of as a store of carbon. When they are burnt to clear land, the carbon turns into carbon dioxide. Globally countries have made agreements to reduce carbon dioxide emissions in an effort to reduce global warming.

A project called REDD (Reducing Emissions from Deforestation and Degradation) allows more developed countries to reduce emissions by buying 'carbon credits' from countries that have large areas of forest. These areas are given a value depending on how much carbon dioxide they could absorb. The idea is that other countries could pay for the credits to offset their own emissions and the money would fund development in countries with forest. In REDD, further deforestation would lose valuable credits. Although REDD is only just starting, in a similar scheme Norway plans to pay US$1 billion to Brazil by 2015 if it reduces its deforestation rate further.

▷ **Eucalyptus are an example of fast-growing plantation trees that can grow closely spaced together and are ideal for producing pulp.**

Debate club

A protected old area of forest has many trees which are in high demand for timber. People in and around the forest live in poverty. Allowing deforestation could create land for farmers and resources for mill owners, and increase economic development. Organise a debate to discuss deforestation in this setting.

You'll need six people to act as the characters who each have a point of view about the pros and cons of deforestation. The rest of the class listen to the speakers in the debate as if they are the government who decide whether or not the forest is exploited.

STATE REPRESENTATIVE

'Selling timber from this forest can pay for regional development. Why should we preserve all the old forest when people here live in poor houses with no electricity or running water?'

ENVIRONMENTALIST

'We must preserve this unique forest. Short-term financial gain is never enough to pay for ecological destruction.'

OLDER WOMAN

'The forest is our larder, our medicine cupboard, and where we have lived for generations. What would we do without it?'

MILL OWNER

'Without access to these trees my factory cannot produce goods cheaply enough to compete with other countries. I'll have to get rid of workers.'

FARMER

'I'm struggling to grow crops on the exhausted fields around my hut. Please let me clear some forest so that I can produce enough food for my family.'

TEENAGER

'I love the forest but I can't bear a life of struggling to survive like my parents. We might all benefit from forestry jobs and better infrastructure if we allow deforestation.'

Glossary

atmosphere layer of gases surrounding the Earth

biodiversity variety of interdependent life forms in a region

biogas gas mostly containing methane formed by bacterial breakdown of organic waste

boreal cold northern region below the Arctic dominated by conifer forest

broadleaved trees with wide leaves rather than needles, such as oak and birch

climate change changes in the world's weather patterns caused by human activity

colonize take over, control and settle on territory away from home. For example, Europeans colonized parts of Africa from the 17th century.

community forest forest maintained by and supplying resources for a local community

conifer type of tree such as pine that has needle-shaped leaves and produces seeds in cones

ecotourism tourism that promotes sustainable use of resources and conservation

emissions release of gases such as greenhouse gases into the atmosphere

export sell and transport to another country

flash flood when a large volume of water suddenly spills onto land

food chain feeding relationships between different living things in a particular habitat

fuelwood wood gathered or cut down to release energy by burning

greenhouse gas gas in the upper atmosphere that warms the lower atmosphere around the Earth by trapping the sun's heat

habitat type of environment where one or several organisms normally live

hardwood dense wood from broadleaved trees including oak and mahogany

hide animal skin used to make leather

hydroelectric system using the force of moving water to generate electricity

infrastructure facilities that serve a community such as roads and water and sewer systems

landslide when large amounts of rock, soil or mud slip down a slope, often causing damage

lichen type of organism comprising both algae and fungi, usually found growing on trees or on walls

logging cutting down trees and stripping them of branches to access their trunks

methane type of odourless gas that may be used as fuel but which is also a greenhouse gas

migrant worker person working away from their home country, often in order to be paid higher wages and send home money to family

old-growth dominated by old, mature trees, dead and alive, from a variety of species

peatland land with generally moist soil rich in peat, which is partly rotted plant remains

photosynthesis process whereby green plants make food for energy and growth from carbon dioxide and water using sunlight

plantation area of land planted with one type of crop, such as eucalyptus or spruce trees

poacher person who hunts illegally on land owned by others

pulp mix of strong fibres extracted from materials such as wood that is used to make paper

regenerated regenerated forest comprises trees that have newly established, sometimes after being planted by people, on deforested land

renewable energy energy from natural sources in unlimited supply such as sunlight and wind

sanitation logging selective logging intended to improve the health of an area of forest

smog polluting mix of fog, smoke and gases that often forms over cities in sunny weather

softwood wood from conifers that is usually easy to cut and less dense than hardwood

subsistence producing or accessing enough food and other basic resources to sustain life for a person and their family

sustainably using natural resources to meet the needs of the present without jeopardising those resources for future generations

taiga boreal forest

timber logs cut and shaped into planks for building

topsoil upper level of soil rich in nutrients that plants need to grow

United Nations international organization promoting peace, security and economic development

woodchip small pieces of wood and bark

Index